2/2³

SESAME STREET®

Celebrating YOU and ME

Many Ways to Be a

FAMILY

Christy Peterson

Lerner Publications ◆ Minneapolis

On Sesame Street, we celebrate everyone!

In this series, readers will explore the different ways we eat, dress, play, and more. Recognizing our similarities and differences will teach little ones to be proud of themselves and appreciate the world around them. Together, we can all be smarter, stronger, and kinder.

Sincerely, the Editors at Sesame Workshop

Table of Contents

All Kinds of Families

A family is a group of people who love one another.

Everyone's
family is special
and unique.

Who is in your family?

Some families live together. Some families live in different places.

My mom and dad live in different homes. I love to spend time with each of them.

Some families are small. Others have many people. Families can have siblings, grandparents, aunts, uncles, cousins, and pets!

Sometimes people in a family look alike. Sometimes they don't.

Elmo's fur is red, and Elmo's mommy has yellow fur!

Some people are born into their families. Other people join their families through adoption or foster care.

There are many ways to become a family, and they all love one another the same!

Families grow and change.

Our family changed when my baby sister was born. Now we have another person to love!

There are many different ways to be a family. The one thing that all families share is love!

19

Proud to Be Me!

Think about the people who love you and care for you. Draw a picture of them!

Glossary

adoption: when a child needs someone to love and take care of them, and a grown-up or grown-ups want a child to love and take care of; they become a family

aunt: the sister of a person's parent or the wife of an uncle or aunt

cousin: the child of an aunt or an uncle

foster care: when a parent is having a hard time taking care of their child, and the child lives with other caring grown-ups who can take care of the child for a while

grandparent: the parent of a parent

uncle: the brother of a person's parent or the husband of an aunt or uncle

Learn More

Bullard, Lisa. *Different Can Be Great: All Kinds of Families*. Minneapolis: Lerner Publications, 2022.

Cipriano, Jeri S. *Getting a New Baby*. Egremont, MA: Red Chair, 2021.

Miller, Marie-Therese. *Parents Like Mine*. Minneapolis: Lerner Publications, 2021.

Index

Photo Acknowledgments

Image credits: Indeed/Getty Images, p. 4; Klaus Vedfelt/Getty Images, p. 4; Thomas Barwick/Getty Images, p. 4; Amrish Saini/EyeEm/Getty Images, p. 6; Attila Csaszar/Getty Images, p. 6; bbernard/Shutterstock.com, p. 6; imtmphoto/Shutterstock.com, p. 7; NDAB Creativity/Shutterstock.com, p. 9; Monkey Business Images/Shutterstock.com, p. 10; DariaBerestova/Shutterstock.com, p. 13; JLco Julia Amaral/Shutterstock.com, p. 14; Shaw Photography Co./Getty Images, p. 15; LumiNola/Getty Images, p. 16; kate_sept2004/Getty Images, p. 18; Geber86/Getty Images, p. 18; Images By Tang Ming Tung/Getty Images, p. 18; Hill Street Studios/Getty Images, p. 19; Inna Kirkorova/Shutterstock.com, p. 20.

Cover images: Rob Marmion/Shutterstock.com; fizkes/Shutterstock.com; 10'000 Hours/Getty Images.

Lerner Publications Company
An imprint of Lerner Publishing Group, Inc.
241 First Avenue North
Minneapolis, MN 55401 USA

For reading levels and more information, look up this title at www.lernerbooks.com.

Main body text set in Mikado. Typeface provided by HVD.

Editor: Brianna Kaiser **Designer:** Laura Otto Rinne

Library of Congress Cataloging-in-Publication Data

Names: Peterson, Christy, author.
Title: Many ways to be a family / Christy Peterson.
Description: Minneapolis, MN: Lerner Publications, 2023. | Series: Sesame Street® celebrating you and me | Includes bibliographical references and index. | Audience: Ages 4–8 | Audience: Grades K–1 | Summary: "Every family is unique, but all families have people who love and care for one another. Come along with favorite Sesame Street characters in celebrating the many kinds of families"—Provided by publisher.
Identifiers: LCCN 2021043432 (print) | LCCN 2021043433 (ebook) | ISBN 9781728456171 (library binding) | ISBN 9781728463728 (paperback) | ISBN 9781728462059 (ebook)
Subjects: LCSH: Families—Juvenile literature.
Classification: LCC HQ744 .P448 2023 (print) | LCC HQ744 (ebook) | DDC 306.85—dc23

LC record available at https://lccn.loc.gov/2021043432
LC ebook record available at https://lccn.loc.gov/2021043433

Manufactured in the United States of America
1-50687-50106-1/28/2022